The Nature of God's Kingdom

The Characteristics of the Kingdom of God

Bisi Oladipupo

Springs of life publishing

Contents

Dedication — V

Foreword — VI

1. Introduction — 1

2. As a Seed — 3

3. Leaven/Treasure — 9

4. Received as a Child — 11

5. We Must Seek It — 13

6. We Must Press Into God's Kingdom — 17

7. Signs and Wonders — 19

8. The Kingdom of God Is Within You — 21

9. Righteousness, Peace, and Joy in the Holy Ghost — 25

10. It Must Be Preached in Power — 29

11. The Love of God — 31

12. The Crucified Life — 33

13. Kings and Priests — 35

14. Everlasting Kingdom — 37

15. Conclusion — 39

Salvation Prayer — 41

About The Author   43

Other Books by Bisi   45

Dedication

To Jesus Christ, my Lord and Saviour—to Him alone that laid down His life that I might have life eternal. To Him that led captivity captive and gave gifts unto men (Ephesians 4:8). One of those gifts is writing!

Foreword

W hen you received your new life in Christ, did you know that you were drafted into another kingdom?

"Giving thanks unto the Father, which hath made us meet to be partakers of the inheritance of the saints in light: Who hath delivered us from the power of darkness, and hath translated us into the kingdom of his dear Son" (Colossians 1:13).

As we are now in a new kingdom, we need to know the characteristics of God's Kingdom and how it works.

Unfortunately, many believers are not discipled after knowing Jesus, which can result in not getting results in many areas of life.

As Christians, we need to know the nature of the new kingdom that we have been drafted into. If you relocated to another country and did not know how things work, you could struggle unnecessarily for a long time.

This book will briefly investigate the nature of God's Kingdom and how it works.

The reader will come away with a greater understanding of the dynamics of God's Kingdom.

THE NATURE OF GOD'S KINGDOM

Bisi Oladipupo

VII

Chapter One

Introduction

So, how can we learn about the nature of God's Kingdom? We need to look from Scripture to explore God's Kingdom. The first place to consider will be the gospels and the various parables of our Lord Jesus Christ about the Kingdom of God. We will extract principles from the parables that Jesus Christ spoke about God's Kingdom. We will also look at other aspects of the Scripture.

So, what is a kingdom?

Many of these phrases will describe what the word "kingdom" means:

- The spiritual realm of God
- A government or country headed by a king or queen; monarchy.
- A political or territorial unit ruled by a sovereign.
- A realm; domain; sphere*

As we discuss the "Kingdom of God", we will settle for the first definition.

The first most important thing is that a person must be born again to see the Kingdom of God (John 3:3).

As citizens of a new kingdom, we need to know the nature of our new kingdom and how it works. This is essential to living a vibrant and effective Christian life.

---

1. *Source (https://www.yourdictionary.com/kingdom

Chapter Two

As a Seed

I n some of the parables that Jesus Christ our Lord related the Kingdom of God to in Scripture, we can see that the Kingdom of God is referred to as a "seed".

Before we look briefly at some of those parables, what is the nature of seed in the natural?

In the natural, if you plant a seed in the right soil conditions, it will grow within time, and eventually, fruit will come forth. I think this analogy about God's Kingdom is essential to understand as this explains why some things take time to manifest. If we don't know that God's Kingdom has the nature of a seed, we can miss it and get frustrated, not knowing that some things take time.

This applies to certain things we ask for in prayer, including our spiritual growth and others. We need to be patient with ourselves and with others. Growth is always a process.

God's Word is a seed.

"The sower soweth the word" (Mark 4:14).

It can take time to bear fruit, just as a natural seed takes time to get roots and begin to grow. There is a reason the Lord Jesus Christ used the analogy of a natural seed to describe the Kingdom of God to expand parallel spiritual realities.

You can find the account of the Parable of the Sower in Mark 4:1-9. When Jesus was alone, the twelve asked Jesus Christ for the meaning of that parable.

"And when he was alone, they that were about him with the twelve asked of him the parable. ¹¹ And he said unto them, Unto you it is given to know the mystery of the kingdom of God: but unto them that are without, all these things are done in parables: ¹² That seeing they may see, and not perceive; and hearing they may hear, and not understand; lest at any time they should be converted, and their sins should be forgiven them. ¹³ And he said unto them, Know ye not this parable? and how then will ye know all parables? ¹⁴ The sower soweth the word. ¹⁵ And these are they by the way side, where the word is sown; but when they have heard, Satan cometh immediately, and taketh away the word that was sown in their hearts. ¹⁶ And these are they likewise which are sown on stony ground; who, when they have heard the word, immediately receive it with gladness; ¹⁷ And have no root in themselves, and so endure but for a time: afterward, when affliction or persecution ariseth for the word's sake, immediately they are offended. ¹⁸ And these are they which are sown among thorns; such as hear the word, ¹⁹ And the cares of this world, and the deceitfulness of riches, and the lusts of other things entering in, choke the word, and it becometh unfruitful"

²⁰ And these are they which are sown on good ground; such as hear the word, and receive it, and bring forth fruit, some thirtyfold, some sixty, and some an hundred (Mark 4:9-20).

So, let us have a quick look at the above. When Jesus responded to His disciples when they asked Him what the Parable of the Sower meant, part of Jesus' first response was "unto you it is given to know the mystery of the Kingdom" (Mark 4:11). In other words, the Parable of the Sower is one of the mysteries of the Kingdom, and I think it is safe to say "the dynamics of the mystery of the nature of seed and how it works".

This simply tells us that the Kingdom of God works like a seed.

If you look at Jesus' responses, they all have natural agricultural implications for the way natural seeds would respond to their environments.

In summary, we find the following about the seed sown:

- Those that fell by the wayside
- Those that fell on stony ground
- Those sown amongst thorns
- Those sown on good ground

As we can see, only those sown on the good ground brought forth fruits. Therefore, the growth condition depends on the ground, which is our hearts, and not the seed. God's Word is described as an incorruptible seed (1 Peter 1:23).

In the Book of Luke, the last verse reads, *"But that on the good ground are they, which in an honest and good heart, having heard the word, keep it, and bring forth fruit with patience* (Luke 8:15).

So, how do we apply this spiritually?

We must cultivate the soil of our hearts if we want to grow and produce fruit. We must guard our hearts with all diligence (Proverbs 4:23). This is one reason we cannot afford to walk in unforgiveness. It will clog up a person's soil. Unforgiveness is not the only enemy to healthy soil; bitterness, carrying on cares, etc., the list goes on.

This is why we are told to "cast all our cares upon the Lord" (1 Peter 5:7). We must also walk in the consciousness that we are dead to sin (Romans 6:11), and God's love has been shed abroad in our hearts (Romans 5:5). We have what it takes to keep our hearts free from clutter and keep it right at all times. We should also remember that we are not living this life alone in our own strength (Galatians 2:20).

Our studying and meditating on God's Word also allow His Word to take root in our hearts, bringing forth a harvest. Therefore, we need to flood our ear and eye gates with God's Word until it takes root and we get the revelation of the Word.

Therefore, one factor that determines growth in this Kingdom is how much attention we give to God's Word and how we cultivate the soil of our hearts. This is the nature of God's Kingdom.

In the Book of Matthew, we find the Lord giving other parables relating to the Kingdom of God by using seed analogy.

"Another parable put he forth unto them, saying, The kingdom of heaven is like to a grain of mustard seed, which a man took, and sowed in his field: Which indeed is the least of all seeds: but when it is grown, it is the greatest among herbs, and becometh a tree, so that the birds of the air come and lodge in the branches thereof" (Matthew 13:31-32).

When we look at big ministries today, they did not start big. They started as a small seed. This is why we need to be faithful in whatever the Lord commits into our hands because promotion comes from being faithful. As we can see from the above parable, it takes time for a seed to grow, so it will likewise take time for us to mature into the things of the Lord. It is when we have grown and passed our tests that the Lord will then commit others into our trust. This is the analogy used in this parable, *"Birds of the air come and lodge in the branches thereof"* (Matthew 13:32). Once again, remember that this started as a seed.

As we begin to mature in the giftings the Lord has given us, get trained, and develop these giftings, the Lord, in due time, will be able to commit more into our hands.

When you look at the epistles, the analogy of a farmer is used, which confirms that God's Word has the nature of a "seed".

"I have planted, Apollos watered; but God gave the increase. So then neither is he that planteth any thing, neither he that watereth; but God that giveth the increase. Now he that planteth and he that watereth are one: and every man shall receive his own reward according to his own labour" (1 Corinthians 3:6-8).

We all know that Paul laboured in God's Kingdom. He said, "I have planted". Isn't that amazing? He knew that he was just part of a greater plan, and things would take time. Has the Lord instructed you to do something, and you think nothing is happening? The concept that God's Kingdom operates as a seed will encourage you.

Your prayers could be seeds for the next generation to reap from. Sometimes, we just plant seeds, and others reap the harvest. The good news is that we will all be rewarded for each part we have played.

Chapter Three

Leaven/Treasure

In the Book of Matthew, we can find another parable relating to the Kingdom of God.

"Another parable spake he unto them; The kingdom of heaven is like unto leaven, which a woman took, and hid in three measures of meal, till the whole was leavened" (Matthew 13:33).

Leaven is something added to bread to make it rise. This process does take time, and if you notice, the above verse says that the woman hid it in three measures of meal. Sometimes, the Lord is doing a work in us. As a matter of fact, the Lord is always at work in us. We need to cooperate with the workings of the Lord in our hearts. Have you had some desires lately? Could the Lord be trying to draw your attention to something He wants to do?

"For it is God which worketh in you both to will and to do of his good pleasure" (Philippians 2:13).

"Again, the kingdom of heaven is like unto treasure hid in a field; the which when a man hath found, he hideth, and for

joy thereof goeth and selleth all that he hath, and buyeth that field" (Matthew 13:44).

The Kingdom which we are now part of is a great treasure. Just as this man gave his all for it, so should we. This is one reason the Bible says that we need to carry our cross and follow the Lord (Matthew 16:24-28). The nature of God's Kingdom takes total commitment to the Lord and His Kingdom.

Chapter Four

Received as a Child

We are warned in the Bible not to despise children (Matthew 18:10). In our society, most countries have policies and legislation to protect children. Why? Because children cannot speak for themselves and are at the mercy of adults most times.

In God's Kingdom, we are told that the greatest person is he, who is like a child. God's priorities are not man's priorities. We can learn great attributes from children.

"At the same time came the disciples unto Jesus, saying, Who is the greatest in the kingdom of heaven? ² And Jesus called a little child unto him, and set him in the midst of them, ³ And said, Verily I say unto you, Except ye be converted, and become as little children, ye shall not enter into the kingdom of heaven. ⁴ Whosoever therefore shall humble himself as this little child, the same is greatest in the kingdom of heaven" (Matthew 18:1-4).

According to Scripture, those that humble themselves as little children are the greatest in God's Kingdom.

So, what can we learn from a little child?

Little children are simple, easy to believe, and have no airs about them. If you notice, the Bible says that we need to be converted and become as little children. This is a process.

"At that time the disciples came to Jesus and asked, "Who is greatest in the kingdom of heaven?" [2] *He called a little child and set him before them,* [3] *and said, "I assure you and most solemnly say to you, unless you repent [that is, change your inner self—your old way of thinking, live changed lives] and become like children [trusting, humble, and forgiving], you will never enter the kingdom of heaven.* [4] *Therefore, whoever [] humbles himself like this child is greatest in the kingdom of heaven"* (Matthew 18:1-4; NLT).

We may not experience some things if we do not change certain things, renew our minds, and stay humble.

Chapter Five

We Must Seek It

To seek is to be intentional. Nobody would stay at home if they were looking for their lost dog. They would go out and look, that is, seek for it.

Although a simple comparison, we must be intentional about seeking the Kingdom of God.

"30 Wherefore, if God so clothe the grass of the field, which to day is, and to morrow is cast into the oven, shall he not much more clothe you, O ye of little faith? 31 Therefore take no thought, saying, What shall we eat? or, What shall we drink? or, Wherewithal shall we be clothed? 32 (For after all these things do the Gentiles seek:) for your heavenly Father knoweth that ye have need of all these things. 33 But seek ye first the kingdom of God, and his righteousness; and all these things shall be added unto you" (Matthew 6:30-33).

In this world, we must be intentional about seeking the Kingdom of God and His righteousness. We must prioritise the things of God's Kingdom. What is God's Kingdom? The things that interest the Lord—getting people saved, sharing the gospel, praying for the sick, and establishing His righteousness. This is where the marketplace ministry comes into effect. The good news is, when we seek, we shall find (Mathew 7:7).

The Lord sometimes places people in strategic positions of influence so that His righteousness can be established. We also all have a ministry of reconciliation (2 Corinthians 5:18-19).

So, how do we keep focused on the things of God's Kingdom? We need to know that the things we see are temporal, and things we do not see are eternal (2 Corinthians 4:18), which will help us keep a proper perspective.

We also need to saturate our environment with the truth of God's Word and His ways. We need to be prayerful and put action to our faith. Faith is acting on what you believe. That could mean many things depending on what each individual is being led to do. We must apply our hearts to the things of God.

The Bible tells us that seeking God's Kingdom and His right-eousness should be our first priority.

During the earthly ministry of Jesus Christ, He preached the Kingdom of God. Jesus Christ, our Lord, also commissioned the twelve disciples to preach the Kingdom of God.

"Then he called his twelve disciples together, and gave them power and authority over all devils, and to cure diseases. ² And he sent them to preach the kingdom of God, and to heal the sick" (Luke 9:1-2).

When Jesus rose from the dead, He was seen by the Apostles for forty days, and one thing that the Lord Jesus Christ did during those days was to preach things about the Kingdom of God (Acts 1:3).

Paul preached the Kingdom of God, and so should we.

"And Paul dwelt two whole years in his own hired house, and received all that came in unto him, 31 Preaching the kingdom of God, and teaching those things which concern the Lord Jesus Christ, with all confidence, no man forbidding him" (Acts 28:30-31).

Chapter Six

We Must Press Into God's Kingdom

W e live in this world, but we do not belong to it (John 17:16). As Christians, we must be intentional about pressing and focusing on the Kingdom of God. The just shall live by faith (Hebrews 10:38) is applicable in not just getting our needs met, but the way we live our lives. Living in the Spirit and walking in the Spirit is a faith walk. As Christians, we are already in the Spirit (Romans 8:9), and as we live in the Spirit, we are to walk in the Spirit (Galatians 2:25).

"The law and the prophets were until John: since that time the kingdom of God is preached, and every man presseth into it" (Luke 16:16).

"The law and the prophets were until John. Since that time the kingdom of God has been preached, and everyone is pressing into it" (Luke 16:6; NKJV)

We have to be intentional and proactive about pressing into the things of God. It does not come by default. You will have to be determined and intentional about it. Nobody will force you to read your Bible and study the Word. If it doesn't get done, only you will reap the consequences and those in your sphere of influence. This is simply because all our actions affect someone else, whether or not we realise it. No one lives unto himself (Romans 14:7).

If you notice, it says, "Every man presses into it". In other words, no one will do it for you. You have to work out your own salvation (Philippians 2:12). The good news is that we are not alone; the life we now live in the flesh, we by the faith of the Son of God (Galatians 2:20), and we can do all things through Christ that strengthens us (Philippians 4:13). All we have to do is to cooperate with the help that the Lord has given us.

This is why all you can do is expose a person to the truth. If you are a leader, teach those that the Lord has committed into your hands the truth. It is now down to the hearers to receive the truth and do something with it. "Every man presses into it"; themselves.

We need to stay focused on the things of the Kingdom of God, even during trials. We must refuse to be distracted. We are told to fight the good fight of faith and lay hold on eternal life (1 Timothy 6:12). It is a walk of faith that takes walking in the Spirit and setting our minds on the things of the Lord. The good news is that the grace of the Lord is sufficient for us, and the Lord is with us, helping us in a mighty way.

Chapter Seven

Signs and Wonders

J esus Christ, our Lord, preached the Kingdom of God during His earthly ministry, with signs and wonders following it.

"40 Now when the sun was setting, all they that had any sick with divers diseases brought them unto him; and he laid his hands on every one of them, and healed them. 41 And devils also came out of many, crying out, and saying, Thou art Christ the Son of God. And he rebuking them suffered them not to speak: for they knew that he was Christ. 42 And when it was day, he departed and went into a desert place: and the people sought him, and came unto him, and stayed him, that he should not depart from them. 43 And he said unto them, I must preach the kingdom of God to other cities also: for therefore am I sent" (Luke 4:40-43).

Verse forty-three above indicates that signs and wonders are part of preaching the Kingdom of God. This includes healing the sick and casting out devils.

This was Jesus Christ, our Lord's commission to His disciples.

"8 And into whatsoever city ye enter, and they receive you, eat such things as are set before you: 9 And heal the sick that are therein, and say unto them, The kingdom of God is come nigh unto you" (Luke 10:8-9).

If you notice, our Lord said to tell people that "the Kingdom of God has come nigh to you". After what? After they had healed the sick. In other words, they tasted the Kingdom of God.

Chapter Eight

The Kingdom of God Is Within You

This is another facet of the Kingdom of God.

During the earthly ministry of Jesus Christ our Lord, the Pharisees asked when the Kingdom of God would come. This is the dialogue.

"[20] And when he was demanded of the Pharisees, when the kingdom of God should come, he answered them and said, The kingdom of God cometh not with observation: [21] Neither shall they say, Lo here! or, lo there! for, behold, the kingdom of God is within you" (Luke 17:20-21).

So, we can see from this scripture that God's Kingdom is also within us.

Christ lives in us

"To whom God would make known what is the riches of the glory of this mystery among the Gentiles; which is Christ in you, the hope of glory" (Colossians 1:27):

Living water flows from our spirits

"*He that believeth on me, as the scripture hath said, out of his belly shall flow rivers of living water*" (John 7:38).

"*He who believes in Me [who adheres to, trusts in, and relies on Me], as the Scripture has said, 'From his innermost being will flow continually rivers of living water*" (John 7:38).'

The Holy Spirit dwells in us

"*16 And I will pray the Father, and he shall give you another Comforter, that he may abide with you for ever; 17 Even the Spirit of truth; whom the world cannot receive, because it seeth him not, neither knoweth him: but ye know him; for he dwelleth with you, and shall be in you*" (John 14:16-17).

We can see from the above scriptures that God's Kingdom is indeed within us. Therefore, we need to live in the consciousness of these spiritual realities.

This will cause our faith to become effective.

"*That the communication of thy faith may become effectual by the acknowledging of every good thing which is in you in Christ Jesus*" (Philemon 1:6).

We need to acknowledge what we have in Christ Jesus.

I remember an incident where a visitor complained of a backache. My husband asked me to pray for her after I had just got back in. In my head, I thought, "I don't think I want to do this now", but I went ahead to pray for this lady. As I laid my hand on her shoulder, she said, "I can feel heat from your hand; something is flowing into me from you". This lady was not a Christian. So, what happened? It was God's Kingdom being released into her, which we all have. I did not feel anything, likewise in the natural, but there was a spiritual transaction. Christ does live in us, and when we minister to others, we are ministering God's Kingdom to them.

Chapter Nine

Righteousness, Peace, and Joy in the Holy Ghost

I n the Book of Romans, the Bible gives us three character- istics of the Kingdom of God.

"For the kingdom of God is not meat and drink; but righteous- ness, and peace, and joy in the Holy Ghost" (Romans 14:17).

In this Kingdom, Jesus Christ our Lord has made us righteous (2 Corinthians 5:21), and we need to live in the consciousness of our righteousness in God. Righteousness is also part of our armour to stand against the enemy (Ephesians 6:14).

As we go about our daily activities, we become aware of our right standing with God. If there is an emergency, you just need to attend to it with the authority that the Lord has given unto us. We are also called to live unto righteousness (1

Peter 2:24). Righteousness and justice *are* the foundation of His throne (Psalms 89:14).

We are also in the Kingdom of Peace; therefore, we should be people of peace. The Bible tells us to follow peace with all men, "Follow peace with all men, and holiness, without which no man shall see the Lord" (Hebrews 12:14). The peace might be afar off, as you can't make peace with everyone, but you can follow peace.

The Lord told us that He has given us His peace (John 14:27) and when we keep our minds on Him, we have access to perfect peace (Isaiah 26:3). Likewise, we have peace with God through our Lord Jesus Christ (Romans 5:1), and as we cast our cares upon the Lord, His peace will keep our hearts and minds intact (Philippians 4:6-7). Sometimes, the Lord also leads us by giving us peace (Isaiah 55:12). Have you ever heard someone say, "I knew I should not have done that as I lost my peace". Being in peace is part of the Kingdom of God.

We don't often encounter the joy of the Lord, but we should do. Joy unspeakable is a tangible experience (1 Peter 1:8). The Lord wants His joy to remain in us and our joy to be full (John 15:11).

A few years ago, a brother shared an amazing experience with my husband and me after a church service. He said that he was in the kitchen at his home with his new child, and suddenly, he saw the Lord Jesus Christ and had an encounter. He shared a few things with us but made a statement that I will not forget. He said, "I was so full of joy that if someone cut off my leg, I would not have felt it". That is what one can call "joy unspeakable which is full of glory". Joy is part of the Kingdom of God.

We all have access to the joy of the Lord, for joy is a fruit of the Spirit (Galatians 5:22).

While the testimony of the joy of the Lord this brother experienced was from an encounter, the good news is that the Lord has given us His joy, which is a fruit of the Spirit.

Chapter Ten

It Must Be Preached in Power

J esus Christ, our Lord, preached the Kingdom of God in power.

"For the kingdom of God is not in word, but in power" (1 Corinthians 4:20).

"And it came to pass afterward, that he went throughout every city and village, preaching and shewing the glad tidings of the kingdom of God: and the twelve were with him" (Luke 8:1).

Jesus Christ, our Lord, also commissioned the twelve to preach the Kingdom of God.

"Then he called his twelve disciples together, and gave them power and authority over all devils, and to cure diseases.

² And he sent them to preach the kingdom of God, and to heal the sick" (Luke 9:1-2).

We must learn how to cooperate with the person of the Holy Spirit to preach this gospel with power.

To preach the Kingdom of God in power, we must know our authority as a believer and be strong in the Lord. Preaching this gospel in power is not for a select few. We are all called to preach the Kingdom of God. That does not mean we will all have a pulpit, but just letting our light shine (Matthew 5:16, praying for the sick in the marketplace and operating in the gifts of the Spirit is bringing God's Kingdom to our sphere of influence).

During the earthly ministry of Jesus Christ our Lord, He said, *"¹⁹ And if I by Beelzebub cast out devils, by whom do your sons cast them out? therefore shall they be your judges. ²⁰ But if I with the finger of God cast out devils, no doubt the kingdom of God is come upon you"* (Luke 11:19-20).

Chapter Eleven

The Love of God

Having a revelation of the love of God is an essential requirement for every believer. As we grow in the knowledge of the Lord, we will grow in knowing His love.

Knowing the love of God, which is in Christ Jesus our Lord (Romans 8: 39), is connected to us walking in all the fullness of God.

"17 That Christ may dwell in your hearts by faith; that ye, being rooted and grounded in love, 18 May be able to comprehend with all saints what is the breadth, and length, and depth, and height; 19 And to know the love of Christ, which passeth knowledge, that ye might be filled with all the fulness of God" (Ephesians 3:17-19).

"17 Then Christ will make his home in your hearts as you trust in him. Your roots will grow down into God's love and keep you strong. 18 And may you have the power to understand, as all God's people should, how wide, how long, how high, and how deep his love is. 19 May you experience the love of Christ, though it is too great to understand fully. Then you will

be made complete with all the fullness of life and power that comes from God" (Ephesians 3:17-19; NLT).

If you notice some of the healings and miracles of the Lord Jesus Christ during His earthly ministry, it starts by saying that He was moved with compassion.

"And Jesus went forth, and saw a great multitude, and was moved with compassion toward them, and he healed their sick" (Matthew 14:14)

The miracle of the multiplication of seven loaves and a few fishes feeding the crowd also started by Jesus having compassion on the crowd.

"Then Jesus called his disciples unto him, and said, I have compassion on the multitude, because they continue with me now three days, and have nothing to eat: and I will not send them away fasting, lest they faint in the way" (Matthew 15:32). The rest of the account can be found in Matthew 15:32-39.

Chapter Twelve

The Crucified Life

I t will take a crucified life to seek the things of the Kingdom of God. So, what does that mean? Leaving behind our own agenda and following the Lord's plans.

Paul put it this way:

"I am crucified with Christ: nevertheless I live; yet not I, but Christ liveth in me: and the life which I now live in the flesh I live by the faith of the Son of God, who loved me, and gave himself for me" (Galatians 2:20).

Allowing Christ to live through us will impact our conduct and way of life. Jesus Christ is about the Father's business, and so should we be. Yielding to the Lord and allowing Him to work through us will result in us not doing our own will but working with Him.

"For we are his workmanship, created in Christ Jesus unto good works, which God hath before ordained that we should walk in them" (Ephesians 2:10).

Chapter Thirteen

Kings and Priests

In the natural, a King has authority, and a Priest stands in the gap for others.

Did you know that in this Kingdom, we have been made Kings and Priests?

"5 And from Jesus Christ, who is the faithful witness, and the first begotten of the dead, and the prince of the kings of the earth. Unto him that loved us, and washed us from our sins in his own blood, 6 And hath made us kings and priests unto God and his Father; to him be glory and dominion for ever and ever. Amen" (Revelation 1:5-6).

So, how do we reign as kings? We use the God-given authority that has been given to us through Jesus Christ our Lord.

We are a royal priesthood (1 Peter 2:9), and we offer up spiritual sacrifices to God through Jesus Christ (1 Peter 2:5).

Chapter Fourteen

Everlasting Kingdom

G od's Kingdom is an everlasting Kingdom (2 Peter 1:11).

"Thy throne, O God, is for ever and ever: the sceptre of thy kingdom is a right sceptre" (Psalms 45:6).

When we become Christians by making Jesus Christ our Lord and saviour, we switch kingdoms (Colossians 1:13). We still live in this world; however, we are in a different kingdom and operate by different spiritual laws. We then have to seek and enforce the Kingdom of God down here. This is one reason the famous prayer, known as "The Lord's prayer", states, *"Thy kingdom come, Thy will be done in earth, as it is in heaven"* (Matthew 6:10).

God's Kingdom is already in heaven, and at the end of our journey in this life as believers, we will be received into His Kingdom (1 Corinthians 15:50). You must be born again to see the Kingdom of God (John 3:3).

Our Lord Jesus Christ, during His earthly ministry, made it very clear that His Kingdom is not of this world.

"Jesus answered, My kingdom is not of this world: if my kingdom were of this world, then would my servants fight, that I should not be delivered to the Jews: but now is my kingdom not from hence" (John 18:36).

Chapter Fifteen

Conclusion

We are in this world, but we are not of this world (John 17:16). We belong to a different kingdom as believers in Jesus Christ, which operates by different rules. God's Kingdom is a spiritual reality, and we need to know how it works to enjoy the full benefits.

We have also seen that we are to preach the Kingdom of God and reach out to others.

We don't need to struggle unnecessarily when we know how God's Kingdom works. Instead, we have seen that we need to cultivate our soil, which is our hearts, to enable us to bear fruit from God's Word.

The Lord has given us authority, and we are kings and priests unto God.

So, let us arise in this great privilege and partner with heaven to say, "Thy Kingdom come, thy will be done on earth as it is in heaven".

Salvation Prayer

F ather God, I come to you in Jesus' name. I admit that I am a sinner, and I now receive the sacrifice that Jesus Christ paid for me.

I confess with my mouth the Lord Jesus, and I believe in my heart that God raised Him from the dead.

I now declare that Jesus Christ is my Lord and Saviour.

Thank you, Father, for saving me in Jesus' name.

I am now your child. Amen.

If you've said this prayer for the first time, send an email to bisiwriter@outlook.com.

Start reading your Bible and ask the Lord to guide you to a good church.

About The
Author

Bisi Oladipupo has been a Christian for many years and lives in the United Kingdom with her family.

Bisi attended a few Bible colleges, and she has obtained a diploma in Biblical Studies from a UK Bible college.

She is a teacher of God's Word, coordinates Bible studies, and has a YouTube channel at https://www.youtube.com/c/BisiOladipupo123.

She writes regularly, and her website is www.inspiredwords.org

Her author page is www.bisiwriter.com

You can contact Bisi by email at bisiwriter@outlook.com.

Other Books by Bisi

The Twelve Apostles of Jesus Christ: Lessons We Can Learn

The Lord's Cup in Communion: The Significance of taking the Lord's Supper

Different Ways to Receive Healing From Scripture and Walk in Health

Believing on The Name of Jesus Christ: What Every Believer Needs
to Know

The Mind and your Christian Walk: The Impact of the mind on our
Christian walk

Relationship Skills in the Bible: Scriptural Principles of Relating to Others